From TIME to TIME

poems

by

JOAN SUTCLIFFE

From TIME to TIME

poems

by Joan Sutcliffe

Published by: In Our Words Inc. /inourwords.ca
Editor: Cheryl Antao-Xavier
Cover image and illustrations: Joan Sutcliffe
Designed by: Shirley Aguinaldo
Author Photo: Honey Novick

Library and Archives Canada Cataloguing in Publication

Sutcliffe, Joan, author
From time to time : poems / Joan Sutcliffe.

ISBN 978-1-926926-81-0 (softcover)

I. Title.

PS8637U832.F76 2017 C811'.6 C2017-902167-2

Contents

Theosophia

Through shadows of the sombre garden
the serpent traces subtle threads

she is Sophia
the soul awakening

too long was she victim
to dark centuries of confusion
that shackled the spirit
with gluttonous clasp

she is Sophia
wisdom of Greece
that shone long ago
in the poet and philosopher
and spoke in the oracles of Apollo

then stilled
in submerging waters of ignorance
she wept countless ages
in confines of constriction
unrecognized, unknown, unwanted

she is Sophia
shamanic spirit
nurtured once in the soul of a people
who held the land in submissive respect
and honoured the essence
of every leaf and stone

she is Sophia
holder of secrets
camouflaged like crystal on fallen snow

imprisoned yet again
behind bludgeoning bars of greed and lust
she has slept the silent sleep of futility
protecting her beauty within her breast

she is Sophia
who is rising again
in mantle of cerulean blue
to weave through worlds
mysterious as midnight

free at last
she is Sophia
wisdom of higher things

Daughter of Capricorn

Have you seen the moon of Capricorn rise
like a goblin's bowl above the hill
luminously white, hauntingly still

when bathed in silver is the landscape
branches encased iridescent in ice
and water surface locked in a vise?

Have you felt the touch of winter's clutch
the air so cold you can hear it crack
so frigid your footsteps leave no track?

Lonely and raw can be the feeling
when no songstress penetrates the night
and tenebrous shadows close in tight

Have you wondered at a Capricorn sky
tremulous of the saturnine tread
pessimistic thoughts heavy as lead?

Yet healing energy fixed at the core
of the gemstone native to this sign
burns lustrous black in the onyx's shine

Have you met the daughter of Capricorn?
Born of the stars dynamic and wise
bound to the earth by mysterious ties

sure-footed she is the mountain goat
silky as flow of upland grasses
secret heart unknown to the masses

Have you seen her climb the rocky slopes
her gaze to the future holding fast
while remaining guardian of the past?

Unfearful of the potent silence
clear to her eye as a crystal ball
she casts her lot where the rune stones fall

Mantled in strength and gentleness
she's protective, as the hard-packed snow
to life that's lying dormant below

Have you known the solace of dark months
when the soul looks deep and love is warm?
That is the spirit of Capricorn.

Imbolc

Subtle the presence of Imbolc
stealing on satin slippers
into the witchery of winter's hold

the dark gate opens
as she ushers in a first pinprick of light
delicate as silver lace

the intangible fragrance of anticipation
thrills through the sleeping silence
and hint of a blush tints the pale stones

as the threshold is crossed
there is no holding back
the old pagan magic rises again

surge of excitement swells
in the bosom of the countryside
stirring into life every seed

in the burning effulgence of candle flame
lit by a thousand devotees
the white goddess returns

Aquarius

White-boned knuckles fracture
the fragments of cracking ice
ripples spread like fluting striations
on black opal
and the eye of Aquarius
scries into stillness of deep waters

A fleeting image
pale as moonlight
deftly eludes the gaze
water is psychic
whisper the pine needles
look and listen

Totem of poet and visionary
a swan glides to the beckon
elongated curve of neck drops
to forage beneath the wavelets
stirring reflections
of a different reality

First song of a wood thrush
breaks through a veil
on the eardrum of nature
trilling loud and long
till the woodlands relinquish
their silence

Hardy little snowdrops pierce
  the compacted earth
drinking in the moisture
  of winter's melting heart
the tang of cool air
  fresh as mint

The wheel turns
  and cycles move on
as the Water-bearer pours
  the age-old ritual
from an ancient world
  into new beginnings

Ides of March

He was a selfish egotist
till one sad night near winter's end
the hand of death passed by his door,
and took away his heart's dear friend.

Nature was at its tenderest
freshly green on maple and larch
but bold dates on the calendar
showed this day as the Ides of March.

His grief was inconsolable,
as the deepest sorrow he bore,
aloud he cried in agony
I curse this day for ever more.

Eclipsing shadows crossed the moon
was someone listening - who knows!
but ever since, the Ides of March
have struck him with life's tragic blows.

He wandered through the world's strange lands
in forests dark and deserts vast
alone and searching restlessly
a soul tormented by the past.

For decades long he roamed the wilds
of who he was he lost all trace
at times he had no food or rest
and never saw a human face.

Once more it was the Ides of March
he turned his eyes towards the west
and to the setting sun he vowed
to start upon a sacred quest.

In caves where shrieking mandrakes grow
and visions rise from tepid streams
he sat in watchful wakefulness
to capture his prophetic dreams.

He searched the shamanic darkness
and killed the demons of his mind
he filled his heart with compassion
all his anger he left behind.

Now he has found the peace within
he knows where his convictions dwell
today it is the Ides of March,
at last he has broken the spell.

Spring Equinox

Eager yet unpresumptuous
expectant yet reticent

like the monk peering out
through the grill in his grey stone cell

thrill of new life hovers
in nature's antechamber

winter loath to let go her stranglehold
retreats slowly into soporific shroud
of invisibility

inky blue softens into creamy curdles
to herald the dripping pools
of luscious return

as early bell summons
the cloistered walk in secluded walls
a wild goose calls

on edge of woodlands
rapturous perfume of the trailing arbutus
pierces the chill
taunting long ascetic solemnity

fresh wind blows crescendo
mounting into anticipation

and restless wings disturb
the unbearable purity
as though to challenge chaste resolve
of the doubting renunciant

there's a promiscuous pause
on brink of euphoria
pregnant with the longing
to break away from monastic silence

the swelling womb bursts
into rush of spring tides
thrusting open the dark oaken gate

and the man in a robe ventures
the world of sun-gilded hearts

River

Ebullient in thrash of melting tides
revelry of river rough-rides the rapids
mimicking the surge of human life

For who has not been swept up
in thunderous roar of swirling current
and left gasping in flood of raw emotion?

Who has not watched the morning mist
lift in gentle spread above the banks
obscuring the city in silent solemnity?

Who has not followed a meandering brook
that drools lethargic in the glades
to where the reeds are murmuring
as loving friends?

Who has not blown their thoughts
into spray of droplets splashing the stones
and mused on words of poetic fancy
that lapse into irony of futile creeds?

And who has not swung high on a bough
across the thrill of cascading chutes
only to fall into troubled pools
of merging throng?

Ice-pure from a mountain spring
the churning river will metamorphose slowly
into tepid waters of sluggard flow
gathering the dust of centuries
the disease, pollution and filth

Just like the spirit of humanity
bearing the weight of civilization
with tears of every world-weary soul
carries its burden
into the sea of infinite life

Beltane

Gatekeepers of the old spirits
shake their magic in broken tins

arousing ancient energies, for
in heartlands of primitive countryside
the father souls have never left

from the woodlands, hills and rivers
lifted on swirls of smoky scent

incessant murmur of pagan chant
calls them to the singing stones
under watchful eyes of the crow

blossoming orchards teem
a shimmering canopy pink and white,

the green man is riding
the wind full of rainfall
to water his seed in softened soil

treading untamed trails of wilderness
the rustic folks still come together

as the May Day fires burn
to enter the secret realms
of gnome and salamander

Soul mates for ever

A haunting scent of pine saturates the air
thrilling every sense
   into tangible anticipation

Déjà vu replays its soliloquy
   tingling shivers into goosebumps,
like sparks leaping from a burning furnace
subtle flashes singe the edge of memory

I see you now the way you were
hands outstretched in greeting
   eyes brimming with tenderness

Soul mates for ever
long separated by thc paths of fortune
but never really lost to me

A solitary lily floats downstream
as notes of Rachmaninov spill
   through an open window
and suddenly I know

Most precious to me is the memory
I'm holding in my heart

Touch of Soul

A stranger's hand reaches out
  intimacy of touch
        transcends the moment

I feel again tender warmth of young skin
as tiny fingers stretch across years
fresh breath on my cheek
as I bend to catch
     the little gasp of ecstasy

then purple-pink runs
through saffron gold of dandelions
field after field
     blooming in midday glory

a checkered dress
sandaled feet
blue eyes reflecting wonder

souls travel through corridors of change
children grow old
parents die
siblings part

friendships are lost in the gnarled fist
of grandfather time
  grasping tenacious
  ravaging memory

like circling wheels we cycle centuries
our pathways cross
      diverge
go round once more
   twice more
     a hundred times more

again, O again!
to meet in the morning sun
a smile or a frown
a curse or a caress

a stranger's hand is
    not a stranger's hand

The Passing

His death was beautiful
still sitting in equipoise of meditation
behind the entrance
where the sunset pours
into the little stone pagoda

the ker-loo-ing call of a crane
broke the silence

for three days he remained
untouched in the gaze of Kwan Yin
his spirit bathed in scent
of ceaseless burning sandalwood sticks

a south wind rose carrying
the exquisite thrill of bamboo flutes
above the persistent chant of
Om Mani Padme Hum

they carried him swaying
across the bridge of woven grasses
to soft green of the foothills
where the plum blossom bloomed
assertive in its fragility

warm breath of early dawn
took the last moisture
lodged in his dry bones

the flames of his pyre
leaped up like dragons
ferocious crimson and tangerine gold
in combat dance of Yin and Yang
the smoke drifted upwards
straight and white

harbinger of a good rebirth
a shower of rain dropped gently
and they said
A great Soul has passed

Winds of Gemini

A gibbous moon rises
like the humpbacked troll
of a Norwegian folk tale
and winds of Gemini blow away
        the clouds

in the clear night air
an old man lays his sleeping bag
        under the stars
to dream the nostalgic longing

for his twin
now waking to the morning song
of a tiny sandpiper
tripping daintily the shoreline
    in the antipodal world

separated always by night and day
they meet only
    in memories that share
the romantic escapades
        of a bygone youth

and live again the rollicking laughter
    of ribald jokes
the evening calm in an old canoe
        paddling the reed-logged inlets

thought swift as Mercury
cloaked in the lightness
   of the winged messenger
transcends distance
   the response instantaneous

closer than the touch of a hand
is the silent communion
   between companion souls

only when the sun has entered again
the house of the Dioscuri
will they come together
   face to face

awake in unison
   to the dawn's precursor
roam the same trails
bathe in the same streams
till the moon has waned
   to its last quarter

Tiny Path

I would take you across the fragile
        bridge of woven grasses
that spans the abyss of despair
  to the shy green of virgin mosses
        centuries in formation

your footstep must be light
  as the feather balance
        on the scales of Ma'at
and your hands gentle
  not to tear apart
        the bryophytic structure

the air is ancient and protective
  absorbing a day's heat
  and reflecting the umber
        of earth tones
            to give a poignant haze

it's the place of visions
        reached only
when peak of your suffering
        dissolves
            into the eye of the storm

and with ears of discernment
  you hear the poetry
        within moaning of the wind

the white walls glimpsed
  through groping tendrils
    are no mirage
  but the home
    of your longing

nurtured in the saddest
    moments of your loneliness

Summer Solstice

A solitary figure in the dusk
  bending over a burning log at the old
    O so old! - hearth stone

though the labyrinth path is no more
  lost long ago in throttle
  of sprawling lilies, lobelia and tangled vine
    he waits

circling in silent witness
giant oaks and full-bodied maple stand
    sharp defined
against deepening violet of summer sky

rustle of a leaf
scurry of night rodent
momentarily disturb the tranquility
an owl hoots -   he strains to listen

soft thud of footfall stirs the grasses
      pulse quickens
      nerves thrill in anticipation
      he calls - once - twice

no one comes
  just a fox - hesitant on the prowl
  or racoon perhaps in scavenger mode
     still he remains alone

so many years have passed away
like dampening of a blaze
        lovers have left - friends flown far
devotees of the circle all gone

scent of smouldering sage recalls
  ceremonies of celebration
        midsummer revelries
                magic and madness
                sacred and profane

excruciating longing invades the scene
  ghosts of regret solidify
              O for one more time!
                one more coming together!

resigned at last
he follows the rituals of the sun
makes offering to east and west
orisons to earth and fire
                lone keeper of the flame

Ghosts

They meet at last
in luscious velvet of summer scent
a sweet clarity in the torrid wilderness

"I have missed you"
she sighs soft as a sylph
caressing the moonlight

"My soul" he replies
purple vines shiver
treble of birdsong thrills the air

They kiss

with the passion of a lifetime's longing
and desperation entombed too lengthy time
in a sepulchre of sadness

Black-eyed and gaunt as the witches of night
he gesticulates madly

*"I have searched for you
in the crevices of my dark dreams
and the cool ripples of dawn's waking"*

Pale faced and delicate as a butterfly's wing
she whispers

"Where were you
when I listened in the cooing
of the mourning dove
and trembling spoke your name?"

She touches his cheek
and two hearts once broken
embrace with tender pathos
spilled in tears of long absence

"O! I have waited the unforgiving distance
stumbling through gloom of centuries"

he howls ferocious as a furnace
destroying the debris of wasted years

"I love you" she says
"for ever and ever
like eternity's reflection burning on water"

They kiss again - lingering - rapacious

with intensity implacable as the pull of tides
tragically beautiful an image caught
in the green plenitude of earth

too brief - then gone
poignancy of ghosts wandering
the grey hordes of lost humanity

The Lodge

Unobtrusive in the erratic chaos
of an abandoned garden
derelict and dusty
it stands long forsaken
to the spirits of forgotten things

assuming a lost elegance
not quite deserted, but woven
into somnolent web of mystery

the door is open
inexplicable longing draws one inside

to gracious splendour looming
from flying dragons and genii
archaic bookshelves hold strange parchments
of thaumaturgic formulae
and age-worn volumes on magic lore,
gold-leafed pages fragile and yellow

the heart lurches
mind falls silent
every sense strains

a limpid air of transparent tranquility
pervades an unnatural lustre
that lacks a human quality
ethereal elements preponderate
tinged with fleeting scent of sandalwood

the house is alive
whispering into the prevailing stillness
ceaseless susurration intensely persistent

though there is no wind
the curtain flutters
the cheek is touched

on periphery of vision
the librarian is glimpsed
ancient, bent, with paper-like skin
moving wraith-like among the tomes,
of sombre yet benevolent mien
a phantom fading in and out

It is a sacred place
to find it, you would be thrice blessed
the busy world passes it by
unnoticed

Canada Day

Dank odours consume
the magnificence of earthy scents
as oak trees cast shadows
  rendering eerie
passage through the woodland trail

birdsong is stilled
to a threatening silence
a blanket of vapours alternates
   hot and cold
      on goosebumps of flesh

the ghosts are all around
ancient souls
Iroquois Algonquin Ojibwe
animal souls
porcupine bear racoon
watching in shades of ether
  just beyond touch on the skin

hurt wounded hunted
memories never silenced
poignant and pregnant in the whisper
  of wind unsettling the leaves

the psychic residue
   of pioneer and quest
lingers in these ancestral forests
 down to the waters
   of the great lake

how many old feet have stood
  on this shoreline
imprinted in the implacable eye
  of centuries
raven   moose   beaver

and last of the French traders
  drawing in their canoe
to the susurrant swash of waves
where spirit voices still speak today

the hauntingly lonely call of a loon
momentarily shatters the dusk
echoing the wilderness heart

taste of wood smoke is on the tongue
  a white egret lands in the reeds
the past merges in the present
          to the future of our land

Thunderbirds

Come, O come, sweet birds of the shadow!
come from beyond the canyons of pain
come, mystical harbingers of hope
and drench these parched furrows with rain.

O come, wild thunder-birds of fury!
fling open the latches on doors of sky
and tear apart the pitiless bosom
to let the waters pour out and cry.

Earth is aching for lack of moisture
the grass is brown as the desert sand
corn husks split and the kernels wither
as sun is scorching a desperate land.

Come, O great birds of ancient glory!
rise from graveyards of ancestral bones
to break this spell of lingering drought
that grinds like steel on crumbling stones.

The dance grows wild, the rhythm more fierce
the ground is shaken by stomping feet
as hard-packed clay is churned into dust
faster, faster the pulverizing beat.

Compulsive drone of drums crescendos
then comes the shriek, shrill cry of joy
as ritual reaches heightened pitch
shamanic spirits enter the boy.

Blanched with paleness, innocent, trembling
lurching the soul into naked fear
while held in grip of holy madness
incantations teem in words unclear.

Suddenly the sun is veiled in darkness
as flapping wings of gigantic span
charge the air with insistent pounding
thrilling the hearts of woman and man.

Storm clouds thick as molasses gather
hovering heavy above the earth
then burst in showers of falling water
splashing like fountains frantic with mirth.

Flowing down hillsides shining and wet
turning the valleys to pools of mud
elatedly splurges the longed-for rain
till streams spill over their banks in flood.

At last the flowers can quench their thirst
the soil expands in satisfaction
as fields and farms and forest trees
enjoy the play of torrential action.

No eye has seen yet the giant birds
whose legend is told in tales at night
but just before a tempest breaks
you can hear the thudding beat of flight.

They come to the call of native song
when the sacred pipe in peace is smoked
and tobacco offered to the fire
and ways of the old ones are evoked.

Impermanence

My life is like the lotus
swelling in copper light of morning
undisturbed by torrents of falling water
that crash into the dark lagoon
where the forest recedes

But my days are ephemeral
as the gossamer thread of the spider
breaking with every twist
and my heart aches to leave
the dearness of faces I know

One day I will drop
into subtle spaces of mind
where fluctuations of familiarity vanish
into splashing waves of impermanence
on the ocean of uncertainty
shifting as phases of the moon

Yet it is the fleeting quality
of a passing breeze
ponderous with scent of lilac
or briefness of the blackbird's song
as evening is lost to night
that gives to each its preciousness

Eternal Egypt

Remember me - I am Egypt
eternal as the amaranthine root
whose breath has seeped into the bones
filling every pore of corporeal longing,
my fires burn still
in seething pockets that lap the corners
of conscious dreaming

I have gone again to my river
where the past has drifted
beyond the bend in the curve,
madcap waves swirl in frothing eddies
at last giving voice
to my sepulchral silence

How I've loved the ibis treading the marsh
where the lotus blushes scarlet
in the morning sun!
Banks once teemed with cries of barterers
scent of cinnamon blending with lilies
priestly linens intertwined
with Phoenician purple of the concubines

My history is immemorial
ever rising like the bird of rainbow plumage
from decadent dregs of burnt out splendour.
But did you ever know the days
of my ancestral glory
when wisdom pressed its soles
on every grass verge
that sprang from newly risen ground?

For millennia I had lain under the water
wrapped in sheets of somnolent obscuration
till my antique heart was woken
my spirit nurtured by astronomer priests
who brought their secrets
from sinking islands of Atlantis
to erect the titanic structures
that grace even yet the sands of Giza

That was the Age of Leo
long, long gone days
steeped in theurgic mysteries
stored in the silent towers of time
within my golden-headed sphinx
veiled in mists of primordial reckoning

Like the swallow's song at sunrise
might pass into sweet music
of the nightingale at evening
to gloss over memories of the day
centuries have flown by swiftly,
and those enigmatic followers of Horus
who looked to the horizon
at the equinox dawn
are now relegated to realms
of fiction and fable

Your scholars delight in exotic dramas
of my Pharaonic dynasties
but do they know of those
who braved the dreadful solitude
deep in the stone interior
of that greatest pyramid
to commune with a world of spirits?

The longevity of my years
has seen the conquest of foreign lands
heroes returning armed with tribute
captive warriors and daughter slaves.
But I am weary of the spoils of war,
fostered in the ancient philosophy
I preach compassion and human love

My life swelled in the souls
that took birth on my precious soil.
Who was ever wise as godlike Imhotep
or beautiful as Queen Nefertiti
ferocious as the fellahin workers
furrowing the alluvial earth
freshly washed by the flooding Nile?

Think of me
when you view the exquisite temple
of my lady Pharaoh
alabaster pillars built into the rock
by her architect lover
for the glory of Amun.
Such a gracious reign was that
rich in arts and blessed with peace!

The sistrums of my sanctuaries
have long fallen silent
as the howl of the jackal
no longer disturbs the necropolis dusk
yet the cool breath of my faithful Anubis
still guides the deceased
through gloomy halls of Amenti
into saffron gardens
where the wheat grows several cubits tall

Listen to me
my spirit persists
like smoke of incense permeating
Luxor's monuments of enormity
luminous once in brilliant colours
carmine red, gold and azurite blue.

In the rubble of my ruins
each shard of pottery holds a memory
awaiting the touch of a master's hand
to be played in full to receptive strangers.
See burial chambers in the Valley of Kings
where painted images vibrate still
to the initial brush stroke
of the scribes of Thoth

Look into my magic that never died
but taps the subterranean waters
of secret brooding,
hearts that weighed heavy
on the scales of Osiris
still haunt the houses of the dead
where sombre tombs
their treasures plundered
corpses violated
carry yet the power of my curses

Today my poppy fields are no more.
Ah, but could you have seen them once
in rippling flow from Thebes to the Delta
like scarlet pools of liquid silk!
O, how their soporific sweetness
enhanced the visions of countless seers!

Now urban culture invades the space
of what was sacred,
yet lovely are the liturgies
of modern Coptic churches
purloined from the mystic rites of Isis,
and holiness pervades magnificent mosques
throbbing in throat of the muezzin
as devotees press their faces
on mosaic tiles

Alas! too many tourists surge my plateaux
for hidden relics of tomb and crypt,
flocking the flamboyance of street bazaars
seduced by scent of spices
and cooling taste of peppermint tea.
I smile at my wicked vendors
peddling pseudo icons of borrowed glory
sculptured in cheap metals and plastic gem

Yet when the Sothic cycle comes full tilt
and a new moon casts a whitened gleam
the pavements crack
to phantom images of my past
then the nightshade demon in my soul
takes flight in sinister capers
to disturb the sleep of the disrespectful

Do not weep for the dreamscape
of my memories
held deep in a bosom that slumbers
but never dies

my occult heart is strong
its immortality sealed
in the burning ankh
embossed on every philosopher's stone

You see me today
in gilded sarcophagi of mummified kings
open to the gaze on museum floors,
in pictorial symbols of hieroglyphic text
indecipherable to the uninitiated,
and in scarab beetles of lapis lazuli
ornately crafted with diligence
by artisans beloved of Ptah

I live on in each re-telling
of legend and myth
remnants of wisdom which had its birth
in my arcane schools of antiquity.
If you keep my peace
in the quiet of your meditations
I will share with you
the secret of my eternal being

The hierophants of my sacred precincts
have long known the truth
of the coming forth by day
for those whose souls are light
as the feather of Ma'at
die only like the moonlight fades
into the crimson meadows
of Ra's return

Leo

Sunlight falls on fading shades
  of the leonine head
turning gold the liquid flow
  of thinning mane
              paler now

as the throaty roar
  is softer too
tragedy of years
  having mellowed the tone

yet lion-hearted still
      the stance
disdainful ever
  of complacent hypocrisy
he remains king
  in the humane jungle of the wise

they told me
  he was once a ferocious hunter
swift and supple to spring
  on churlish cults that batter reason
  self-indulgent systems that fail
                  the underprivileged

a solitary beast
      noble and just
championing the field
  of lost causes

I met him long ago
  old even then
silver-haired and gentle
                    as moonlight

steeped in the knowledge
  of ancient sages
protector of all that is precious
now as yesterday
  he is still my teacher

July showers

Water drops slowly
off the pine needles
down my long nose
deliciously wet on my cheek

stimulatingly green the forest steams
scarce a hair's breadth apart
we stand

you look so funny
old sou'wester
clomping boots
I would burst out laughing
if my heart didn't ache so

a squirrel leaps
branch sways
dropping a deluge

caught by surprise
we jump
our shoulders touch

sun breaks through
sparkling on tiny balls of moisture
a bird sings in ascending scale
unspoken there's a tremble
in the meeting of our eyes
Shall we continue our walk?

descant from far woods
dichotomy of motifs
thrown to and fro across the distance
Hear the little warbler singing to its mate!
I would sing too
but for the lump in my throat

suddenly
another swift downpour
we seek shelter in a make-shift lean-to

so close together
I can see the break of colour spectrum
in the droplets
on your lashes

is there anything so beautiful
as a rainy day in July?

Lammas

The ghost of Ceridwen walks tonight
  at moonrise on the eve of Lammas
black shadows fall in the cypress grove

it's the time of the raven's flight
  peak of the peach harvest
   and the cutting down of fields

we cry for the dying corn god
  as the sorrow of Cybele
  once shook hillsides of Samothrace
fertility's offering to sacrifice
  at turning of the year

It's the night of ancient feminine wisdom
  that holds the world
   in the cauldron of its womb
to pass through gates
        of death and resurrection

as naked warriors once laid down
their shields by south-west waters
and the white-robed virgin
    set free the dove

On either side, summer plays still
  in the rushing stream
  in sound of woodlands
      as soughing wind stirs softly
          through the trees

but the hours will let gently go
  buzz of bees in foxglove's bell
  constant click of crickets in the grass
  needle-thin hover of dragonflies
        sapphire blue with gossamer wings

imperceptibly the days will shorten
  and lazy heat bend to fall tides

Dreamer

Sleep where the jaguar roams
remote in jungles of Guatemala
choose a grass-covered mound
where the silent towers
loom above swaying treetops

touch your forehead to rock
weathered by centuries' standing
and dream in the cradle
of your antique heart

You were there
when rain gods drenched the soil
and the maize grew tall

when the dyes were mixed
you wore crimson threads of Mayan weaving
played the ritual of ceremony
and you sang the words of peace
as kings mixed blood with the earth

you were the white virgin revered as holy
the gnarled peon labouring the fields
and shredding vines
beater of metal into golden plate
and carver of history on stairways of stone

you climbed the pyramidal heights
to see the land as a silken flow
of gossamer gauze
in emerald green of wild fertility
and watched as summer turned to fall

Wake up sweet dreamer
your visions of night fade
with the morning star

as strange dimensions intertwine
between the cracks of time

Elegy on a Hilltop

Jim and Dyanne
from Suzy and Sierra

In the shadow of our sorrow
  we sit together
face to face with the implacable boatman
who ferries the waters
  of the great mystery

holding our loss so deep inside
we touch the nadir of the circle
  moonless night of the heart

time stretches like wings of a great bird
    still we sit
till dawn flecks pink with blue
urging through the sweet grass
  scent of mist rising

a gentle father, a spirited mother
  whimsical grandparents
our memories spoken aloud
  then released
into solemnity of shared silence

O the inexplicable healing
sitting together in this sacred space
  sunlight warm on the skin!

Mountains and Lake

inspired by a painting of Lauren Harris

He laid his canvas bare to the elements
the air so pure
he felt the spirit of quiet brooding
lurking in nature's waiting room
just beyond reach of tangibility
its image mirrored in waters lying limpid

with liquid fluency of brush and pigment
he has captured an ethereal fire
that burns with the golden effulgence
of immaculate light

indifferent to human desire
mountains white as alabaster vases
soar to the ultimate pitch
their music falling like solar sparks
to stir into effervescent wavelets
the silky surface of aqua blue

how blessed is this land
untouched by mundane longings
to tamper with flow of untamed creativity

silent, aloof and lonely

Envelope

A love letter sealed in a violet envelope
crosses turquoise waters
    of a tropical sea

rocks on trans-continental rails
    by day, by night, by day
lulled in monotonous sway
    rattle and clatter

words of tenderness
written with flourish of cursive script
    beg forgiveness, hope, assurance
    unbreakable remembrance
a messenger from the heart

someone is waiting
    with mild desperation
tides ebb and flow
    between miles of separation
seasons have passed
    from winters to spring

so near it draws now
chug-a-chugging through valleys
    of sweet blowing grasses
that longed-for harbinger
    of reconciliation

But - O so tragic!

a thunderous roar
the hillside cracks
a landslide hurtles
    its debris and rubble
burying the train with all aboard

and a little violet envelope
    is lost forever

Groundhog Hill

For Alan

1935 – 2008

Humanitarian and friend of all wildlife

Engraved on copper the words speak
to the stag's aloof ascending
where the trail is steep
solitary and meandering
and cornflowers spread unending

Your bench of cedar gazes far beyond
the crimson forest's susurrant sway
of birch and maple treetops
to charade of shattered light at play
on the horizon's distant looking-glass

Sneaking unawares this precious hilltop
past furtive eyes of a fox, and surge
of monarch butterflies
your little granddaughter breaks the peace
tickling faces with purple phlox

Ceremony and offerings
blend with scent of burning sage
a loud staccato call of a crow
shamanic and significant
splinters the valley in jagged echo

Your spirit inhabits this sacred space
where time and timeless meet
subtle as the flow of air
mysterious depths unfathomed
shift the features on memory's face

Dearly loved by all of us
white tears wrapped in a leaf
never to be forgotten
the hawk hovers above you
the groundhog burrows beneath.

Milkweed

Pale flaxen threads like silky soft hair
catch the light of Indian summer
as the crisp knotty pod cracks open
to scatter a thousand wispy seeds into the wind

She is the milkweed plant
wild child of nature
nurturer of butterflies and gatherer of pollen

She is in tune with shamanic secrets of the seasons
as to when the lily-of-the-valley will proliferate
spilling its perfume recklessly through the fields,
how the poignancy in the song of the wood thrush
can foretell the rainfalls of spring,
at the first touch of warmth she can count the days
to the blossoming of the orchards

If she sees the hawk hover above the open spaces
she knows there will be a loss
and retreats into the incognito of obscurity
bowing her head among the fringes of forest ferns

She is a friend of the beetle and the groundhog,
the swallow and the untamed wilderness
she flourishes in the moist heat of day
and stands hardy in the cool night air

As the taste of metal taints her sap
and a dank odour dulls the summer scents
she recognizes the portent,
something is dying
a body sinking into waters of Lethe
but a soul aflame with longing
struggling on brink of expansion

Just then a sunray falls on royal purple
of flowering buddleia
and she smiles with certainty
a monarch butterfly has left its cocoon

The Inner Voice

The voice may come at any time
in the opulent splendour of a tropical night
or the crude light of dawn
striking chill pavements of a city slum

it may come in sharp staccato of sound
that makes you look around
when no one is there
or unspoken
out of the subtle lining of mind
in still spaces between thoughts

it may come when you least expect
airy as a feather stroking
outermost strands of hair
yet intense as a shock-wave
rippling through your whole being

it may come
as a twitch of meaning emerges
in sudden rustling of a leaf
shy as the sandpiper's tweet
aloof as the whip-poor-will
calling through cedars

it is the voice of your true home
the nostalgia that never left you
even in the darkest despair
of your addiction
to the lethal waters of forgetfulness

it may make you squirm
in the power of its insistency
but this is you
in the essence of who you are
and you cannot break free
not even in dying

you will only fall into the great silence
from which you came
and it will push you back
into the maelstrom of churning

you will open your eyes
to the same earth
nothing has changed
humanity still holds you in its palm
compulsive drone of cicadas still thrills
the summer evening
and the voice will come again

Remembrance Day

Rocked in rattle of shivering bones
wearing pallor of intense fatigue
a soldier is dying

scent of jasmine saturates his senses
soporific sweetness indulging
the chaos of exotic dreams

visions that lead into gigantic jungles
of melting candles pouring flames
into the throbbing skull

perpetual insect buzz crescendos
into roaring force
of blood-sucking swarms

hot fumes hang heavy
in humid folds of black night
gaseous as the fever-infested swamps

he gasps for water
to ease the unquenchable thirst
and drops into a pit of memories

chill damp of proliferating sweat
overwhelms a burning body
until the spirit rises

to walk out into stillness
of cool moonlight
mirrored on a tranquil sea.

We will never know, will we?

Desolate - O so desolate!
silent the lonely roads bristle,
ominously lugubrious
the wind has dropped to a whistle.

Remote of human habitation
no soul is walking the linnet's thread
where gnarled old oaks bend like an arch
to tunnel the twisting turns ahead.

Each bend reveals a hollow blackness,
no penumbral shadow lightens the fall
of what is pulled towards the vortex.
Grim expectancy hangs like a pall.

Hiss and crack of electric charge
fire a strange metallic glistening
that tenses the nerves to breaking point.
Something unearthly is listening.

Startlingly sudden the engine stops,
the car falls dead - no groan - no spark,
gliding like a somnambulist
the passenger's lured into the dark.

A flash of purple - a shining disk
swooping and lifting like a hawk,
spinning like the ecstatic dervish
more blinding than a lightning fork.

A giant figure seems to beckon,
void eyes with glaucous coating smeared
fill an instant the way in front, where
the ill-fated one has disappeared.

Then stillness bathes the countryside,
a tranquility - soft - unspoken
yet unknown hours have passed in blankness.
Tomorrow's dawn's already broken.

Rumours are raging rampant and wide
of a lambent saucer circling low
weaving ethereal images
in the fields where the wheat crops grow.

In mysterious roads of no return
touches of memory may still be,
somewhere a traveler's lost in time.
What happened we'll never know, will we?

Sacred Samhain

Oak leaves tremble into brittle fall
as chill winds shake the hill
suddenly the hollow tap-tapping
of the woodpecker is still

this is the sacred night of Samhain
when the veils between worlds are thin
and across dark waters of Lethe
the chimes of phantom bells begin

ancient shadows of those long dead
held still in the bosom of earth
precipitate into visions that leap
over chasms preceding this birth

like bursts of crepitating bubbles
in transient flight they move uncertain
so many baleful yellow ghosts
on either side the parting curtain

plangent relics of old sorrows surface
in surges of hot weeping
then slip through fingers faltering
mercifully drowned in sleeping

silvery shifts the moonlit sky
to reveal a chink in the cloud
dropping the secrets of Samhain
white pearls from a shallow shroud

only a moment the door is opened
the mind blown wild with delight
as spirits whisper to receptive ears
silently slips by the night

Who comes a-knocking at the door?

Night whispers its secrets
there's a knock on the door

will you open it
let enter the stranger
in a coat that is black
yet reflects the light of a virgin moon?

could be an angel
or a demon in disguise
you can't always tell from a furtive feature
or a stoop of the shoulders

the first words to greet your ears
could moisten your eyes
for their tales of sadness in a world of suffering

or you might laugh
to hear of the clown with a nun on his back
carrying his burden
from the sublime to the ridiculous

don't be fooled by a soft lilt in the voice
you have to listen in the silence between syllables
to catch the warmth of spontaneity
or the vile chill of hypocrisy

gaze keenly through inner perception
look beyond grimace and grin
and still the beat of anticipation

a saint may ask
for your most precious possession
will you refuse?

the dark one may offer you
what you most long for
will you accept?

just stand in the innocence of your purity
and open the door

FROM TIME TO TIME

White bark is stripping from the birch
tenderly he tears loose and folds
gnarled fingers shaping
each piece inside the other
to write his story in symbol and glyph

a flash of sunlight splurges from cloud
catching the furnace blaze of copper
that bursts into shaking mops of saffron glory

and his world is lit with immaculate glow
of unpromised expectation
"*I am young again*," he whispers
as he wraps himself
in the wisdom of his years

first stroke from the quilled feather
dipped in the inks of nature's juices
scratches the sign of earth and water

He remembers the days of Gilgamesh
the magi of Chaldea
the philosophers in the schools of Greece
Sufi dancers in ancient Persia

He was a poet in the cafés of Montmartre
a singer of Beethoven's *Ode to Joy*
a soldier on the battlefields of Europe
a pilgrim to the temples of Tibet

The long night is passing
yet time is illusive as a breath in the mist
another winter solstice dawns
as his midnight watch is broken
by rising sun in Capricorn

The parchment has grown brittle
as the fingers that shape the memory
the ink has run dry
the last words hover unformed, unwritten
to find their home
in the silent records of eternity

You are You

The lilacs are falling
though their scent still pervasive
is succulent and moist

now, lachrymose purple of sunset
drips into lingering red
tinged with unbearable poignancy

a tanager remains singing
before the long solitude
and you whisper "I will remember"

but your rest in the pelagic waters
of dreamless sleep is so deep the ripple
of cognizance passes you by

a slumber so intense the soul escapes
to commune with the mystery
of its own ontology

as though from the night of centuries
dawn of return swells slowly
bleaching the shades of non distinction

on immediacy of waking
there is no memory
no language, no urgency

just the essence of your clarity
pure as stretch of a virgin meadow
and you whisper "Who am I?"

in the silence of being
without words, just knowing,
only for that instant you are YOU

then you whisper “I remember
I have been here before”
and the lilac is blossoming again

www.ingramcontent.com/pod-product-compliance
Ingram Content Group UK Ltd.
Pitfield, Milton Keynes, MK11 3LW, UK
UKHW020138250726
13967UKWH00002B/726

9 781926 926810